S0-AYA-452
Roanoke County Public Library
Vinton Branch Library
800 East Washington Ave.
Vinton, VA 24179
NO LONGER PROPERTY OF ROANOKE COUNTY LIBRARY

Descendants of Darkness™

0 1197 0629534 0

Yami no Matsuei

11

Story & Art by Yoko Matsushita

Descendants of Darkness
Yami no Matsuei
Vol. 11
Shôjo Edition

Story & Art by
Yoko Matsushita

English Adaptation/Lance Caselman
Translation/David Ury
Touch-Up & Lettering/Gia Cam Luc
Graphics & Cover Design/Courtney Utt
Editor/Nancy Thistlethwaite

Managing Editor/Annette Roman
Director of Production/Noboru Watanabe
VP of Publishing/Alvin Lu
Sr. Director of Acquisitions/Rika Inouye
VP of Sales & Marketing/Liza Coppola
Publisher/Hyoe Narita

Yami no Matsuei by Yoko Matsushita © Yoko Matsushita 2000. All rights reserved. First published in Japan in 2001 by HAKUSENSHA, Inc., Tokyo. English language translation rights in America and Canada arranged with HAKUSENSHA, Inc., Tokyo. New and adapted artwork and text © 2006 VIZ Media, LLC. The DESCENDANTS OF DARKNESS logo is a trademark of VIZ Media, LLC. The stories, characters and incidents mentioned in this publication are entirely fictional.

No portion of this book may be reproduced or transmitted in any form or by any means without written permission from the copyright holders.

Printed in the U.S.A.

Published by VIZ Media, LLC
P.O. Box 77064
San Francisco, CA 94107

Shôjo Edition
10 9 8 7 6 5 4 3 2 1
First printing, May 2006

For advertising rates or media kit, e-mail advertising@viz.com

www.viz.com

store.viz.com

PARENTAL ADVISORY
DESCENDANTS OF DARKNESS, YAMI NO MATSUEI, is rated T+ for Older Teen and is recommended for ages 16 and up. This volume contains violence and mature situations.

Table of Contents

Chapter 46 3
Chapter 47 34
Chapter 48 57
Chapter 49 77
Chapter 50 101
Chapter 51 121
Chapter 52 138
Chapter 53 157

ONLY MOMENTS AGO...
A WORM-HOLE BURST THROUGH THE FORCE FIELD THAT SURROUNDS KURIKARA'S REALM...
...CREATING A TINY RIP IN IT.
SOON AFTER THAT...
Descendants of Darkness
闇の末裔
やみ まつえい
CHAPTER 46
IN THE LOWEST LEVEL OF TENKU'S CASTLE, THE BORDERLAND GUARD'S WATCH ROOM...
BEEP
BEEP
BEEP
BEEP
WHAT THE--
!!!
GUARD
AAH!

SORYUU...

I'VE BROUGHT YOUR TEA.
AH, YES.
THANK YOU.
I KNOW YOU'RE BUSY, BUT YOU REALLY SHOULD TAKE A BREAK.
SWP
IT'S ALL RIGHT. THIS IS MY JOB.
Wants him to get married and settle down
KIJIN MAY BE ALL RIGHT ON HIS OWN, BUT I FEEL BAD FOR TENKO.
Sigh
SHE'S AT AN AGE WHERE SHE NEEDS A PARENT'S ATTENTION.
Old people never stop nagging...
He's thinking, "Here we go again!"
Hmm...
I DO FEEL BAD FOR THEM.
BUT MY CHILDREN ARE JUST LIKE ME.

ON THE DAY I FOUGHT KURIKARA ...
...THE EMPEROR GAVE ME A SMALL PORTION OF HIS POWER.
BUT IT WAS SO BIG ...
...SO HEAVY.
THE EMPEROR'S STRENGTH OVERFLOWED, POURED OUT OF MY BODY, AND FLEW INTO THE SKY. THAT'S HOW KIJIN WAS BORN.
THEN IT FELL INTO THE SEA AND MADE TENKO.

MY POWER EXCEEDED ITS LIMIT AND SPLIT INTO TWO SEPARATE CONSCIOUS ENTITIES...
...TENKO AND KIJIN.
OUR BODIES MAY BE SEPA-RATE, BUT...
...WE SHARE THE SAME HEART.
I'M SURE THEY UNDER-STAND.
I SUPPOSE YOU'RE RIGHT.
I'VE SAID TOO MUCH.
PLEASE FORGIVE ME, SORYUU.
SORRY TO INTER-RUPT AT THIS LATE HOUR!!!

SORYUU!
THE FORCE FIELD THAT HOLDS KURIKARA IN THE FUYUU DESERT HAS BEEN BREACHED!
?!
WHAT?!
EVEN THE TINIEST RIP COULD ALLOW KURIKARA TO ESCAPE!
THE IMAGINARY WORLD IS ALREADY UNBALANCED! IF HE STARTS ANOTHER WAR, IT COULD MEAN OUR DESTRUCTION!
SORYUU!!

SORYUU, WAIT!
YOU CAN'T GO OUT IN PUBLIC LIKE THAT!
WHUP
AT LEAST LET US BRAID YOUR HAIR!
I DON'T HAVE TIME FOR SUCH NONSENSE!!

VEEN

...

I KNEW THE FORCE FIELD WAS GROWING WEAK, BUT...

...WHO COULD'VE--

KURIKARA, YOU BASTARD!!!

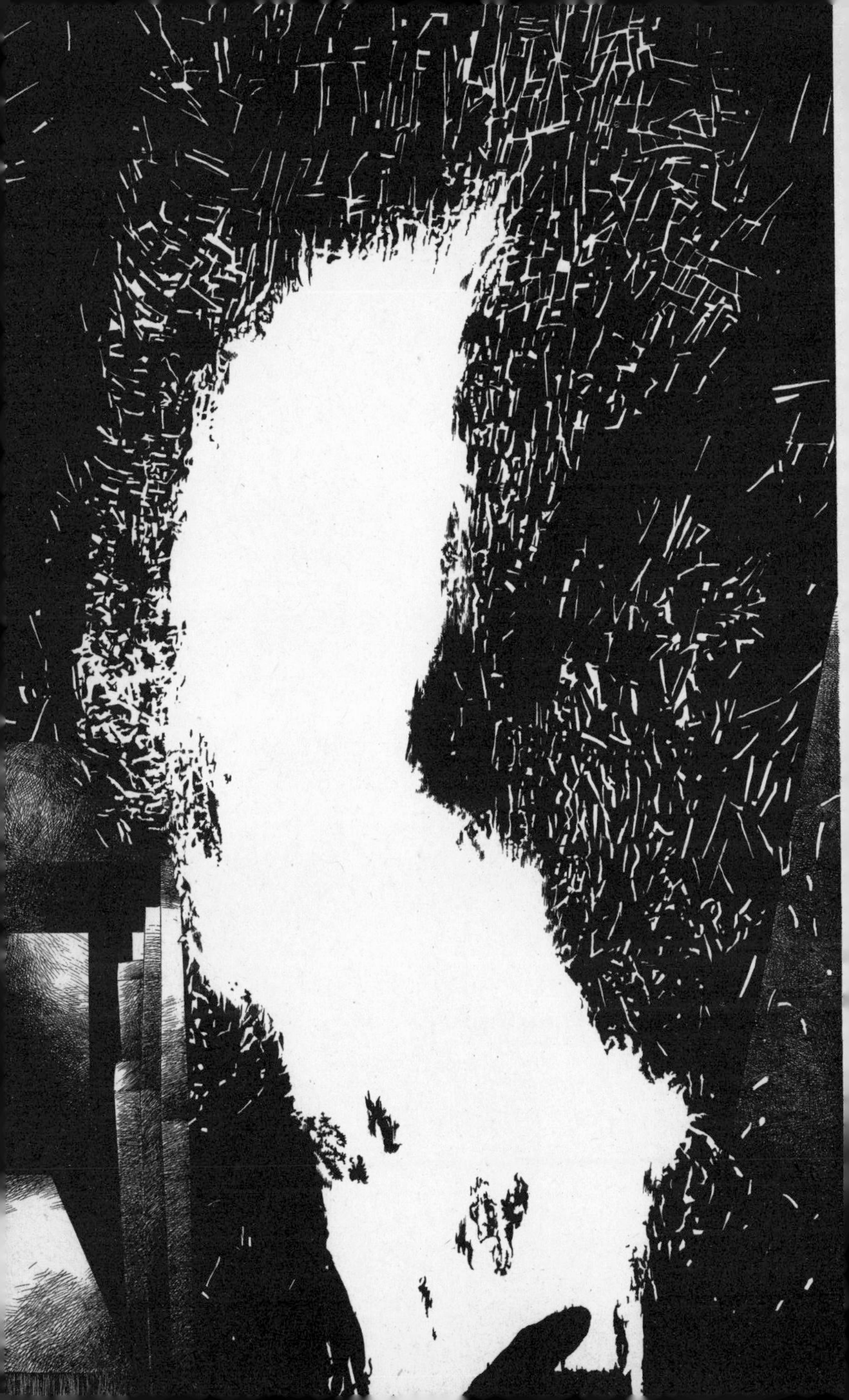

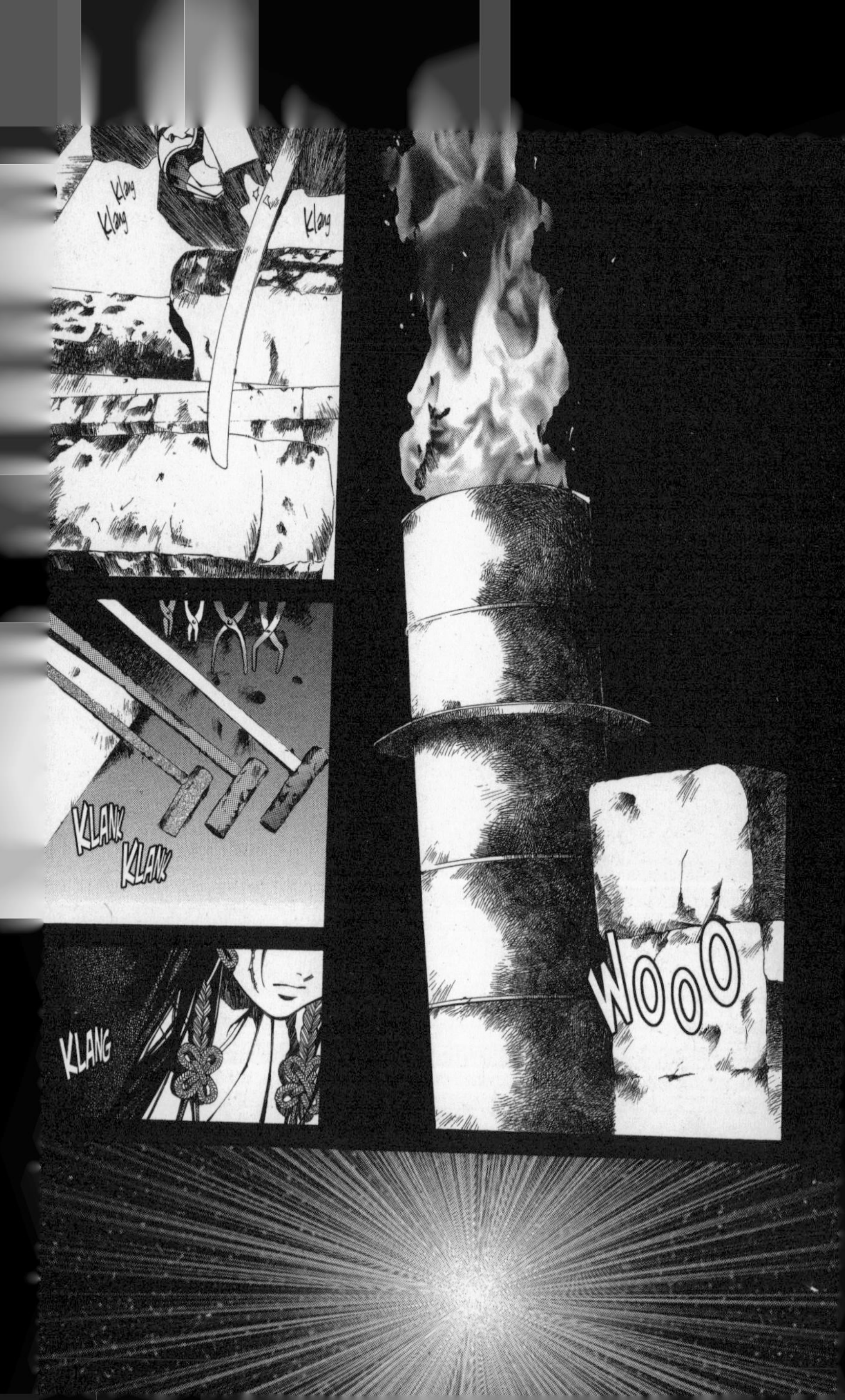
Klang
Klang
Klang
KLANK
KLANK
KLANG
WOOO

KLANNG
KLANG
KLANG
KLANG
FSHHH
KRK KRK
Splash

...
!!
THE SPIRIT OF FUTSU?

闇(やみ)の末裔(まつえい)

DESCENDANTS OF DARKNESS
YAMI NO MATSUEI

I AM THE SPIRIT OF FUTSU.
I AM KURIKARA'S NUMBER-ONE SWORD, AND ALSO HIS RIGHT-HAND SERVANT.
IF YOU'VE COME TO DESECRATE THE SACRED BLACKSMITH'S FORGE WITH YOUR GREED, LEAVE NOW!
IF YOU DON'T, YOUR LIFE WILL BE FORFEIT!

WOOO
MAKE YOUR CHOICE! LIFE...
...OR DEATH?
H-HOLD ON!
I JUST WANT TO SEE KURIKARA, THAT'S ALL!
THROB THROB
THE KING OF THE DRAGONS HAS LOCKED HIMSELF IN THE FORGING ROOM OF THE BLACKSMITHS.
NO ONE MAY SEE HIM NOW.
A SMITHY?
KURIKARA IS A FIRE SHIKI, BUT HE'S ALSO THE GOD OF SWORD-MAKING.
Yeah.
I'VE HEARD OF IT.
That's pure fiction.
APPARENTLY IT WAS HE WHO FORGED ALL THE FAMOUS SWORDS OF JAPANESE MYTH.
YES, THEY WERE ALL MADE BY THE DRAGON KING.
ANCIENT WRITINGS
HE CREATED ME TO BE HIS RIGHT-HAND MAN.

ANYONE WHO WOULD DESECRATE THE FORGING ROOM IS AN ENEMY OF THE DRAGON KING!
IF YOU WANT TO SEE THE DRAGON KING, YOU'LL HAVE TO DESTROY ME FIRST.
WHUP
WHAT ?!
THERE-FORE...
...I MUST ELIMINATE YOU.
WAIT! I DON'T WANT ANY TROUBLE!
IF YOU WANT ME TO WAIT TILL HE'S DONE FORGING, THEN I'LL WAIT!
DISCUSSION IS POINTLESS!!
WAAAAH!!
Why does this always happen to me?

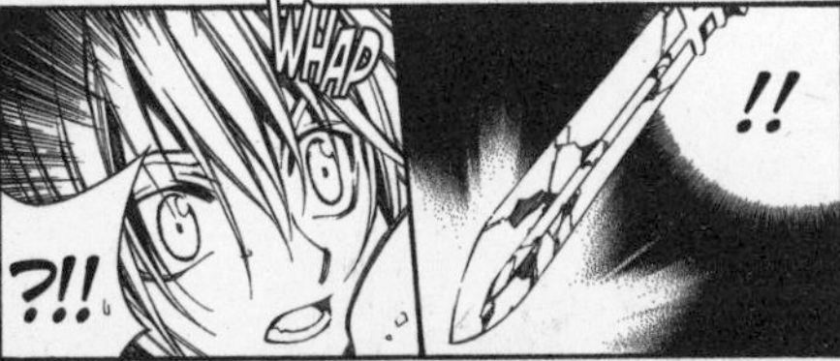

I DON'T REMEMBER ASKING YOU TO DO THIS.

I'M SORRY. I WAS ONLY--
All right...
THAT'S ENOUGH. GO AWAY!
KURIKARA ...

SO THIS...

THIS IS THE LEGENDARY DRAGON THAT FOUGHT SORYUU AND BURNED THE IMAGINARY WORLD...

...KURIKARA, THE KING OF THE DRAGONS?!!

FWUP

TMP
WHAT?! HE'S JUST A LITTLE KID!!
NO!!
IT CAN'T BE!
GRR...
DON'T BE RUDE !!
You're just a kid too!

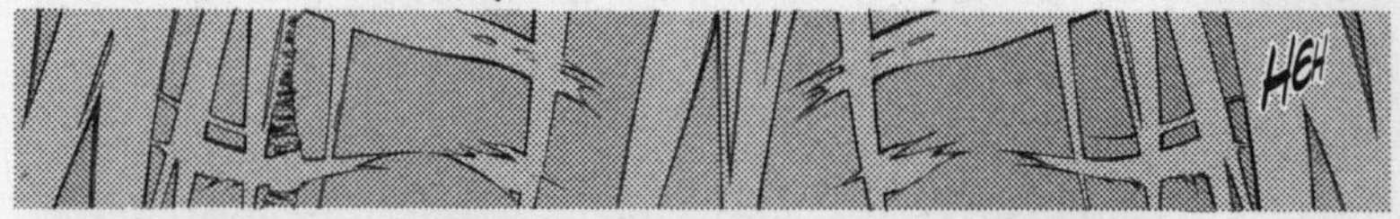
HEH

WELL, IF YOU'RE SOMEONE WHO JUDGES THINGS BY THEIR APPEARANCE, THEN...
...YOU REALLY ARE A CHILD.

I DON'T KNOW WHY YOU CAME HERE, BUT...
...YOU'D BETTER LEAVE NOW. I'M BUSY.
WAIT, KURI-KARA!!
PLEASE ALLOW ME TO CHAL-LENGE YOU!!
I NEED YOUR POWER!!
I THINK NOT.

I DON'T LIKE HUMANS.
AND I'M EXTREMELY IMPATIENT.
TMP
THIS IS YOUR LAST WARNING...
GO!!
B-BUT ...!!!
NO WAY!!
GRR
Hisoka's looking good.
Well, if he hates humans, what can we do?
Hmm...
ISN'T IT NICE TO KNOW WHERE YOU STAND WITH HIM?
Kinda?
HOP
HOP
SAY SOME-THING, YOU BASTARD!!!
TMP
DO YOU THINK I CAME ALL THE WAY HERE TO BE TURNED AWAY?!
YOU'RE NOT EVEN LISTENING TO ME! WHAT'S WITH THE ATTITUDE?!
MAYBE YOU THINK I'M NOT WORTH CHALLENG-ING?!!

!!
FWASH

THANK YOU!

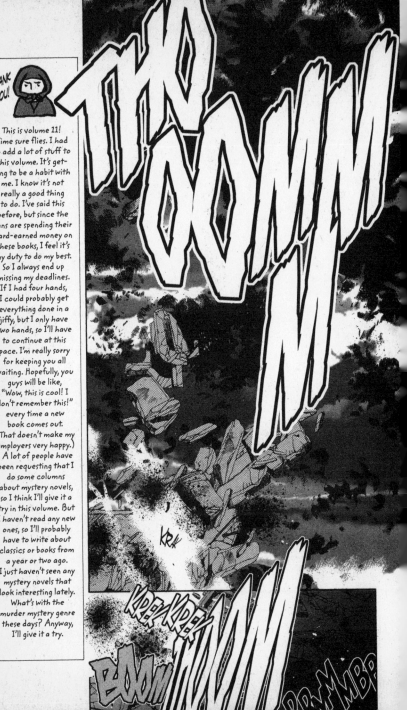

This is volume 11! Time sure flies. I had to add a lot of stuff to this volume. It's getting to be a habit with me. I know it's not really a good thing to do. I've said this before, but since the fans are spending their hard-earned money on these books, I feel it's my duty to do my best. So I always end up missing my deadlines. If I had four hands, I could probably get everything done in a jiffy, but I only have two hands, so I'll have to continue at this pace. I'm really sorry for keeping you all waiting. Hopefully, you guys will be like, "Wow, this is cool! I don't remember this!" every time a new book comes out. (That doesn't make my employers very happy.) A lot of people have been requesting that I do some columns about mystery novels, so I think I'll give it a try in this volume. But I haven't read any new ones, so I'll probably have to write about classics or books from a year or two ago. I just haven't seen any mystery novels that look interesting lately. What's with the murder mystery genre these days? Anyway, I'll give it a try.

KRAK
KRAK
KRASH
HUH?
WHAT'S THAT?
OH NO! IT LOOKS LIKE IT'S BEGUN!!
LOOK OVER THERE!!
EVEN FROM THIS DISTANCE, I CAN FEEL THE POWER OF THE DRAGON KING CRUSH-ING ME!
WE PROMISED THE MIKO...
...THAT WE'D BRING THE BOY BACK UNHARMED.

WOO OO

KRAK KRAK
OH...
HMM...
SO YOU'RE STILL ALIVE. YOUR DEFENSIVE POWERS WERE BETTER THAN I THOUGHT.
HISOKA!!
SSSS
WHAT A TERRIBLE THING I'VE DONE TO YOU, YOU POOR HUMAN BOY. THE PAIN OF THOSE BURNS MUST BE HORRENDOUS.

I'LL END YOUR MISERY ...
...OUT OF KIND-NESS.
...
FUTSU!!
WHUP

YOUR POWERS ARE NOTHING COMPARED TO MINE.
EVEN THE SHINIGAMI OF THE KING OF HADES ARE NO MATCH FOR ME.
YOUR WOUNDS WILL OOZE PUS AND ROT. YOUR SKIN WILL FESTER AND THE OVERWHELM-ING PAIN WILL DRIVE YOU MAD.
SO, TO SPARE YOU THAT, I'M GOING TO KILL YOU.
FUTSU...
OF ALL MY CREATIONS, YOU ARE THE ONE CLOSEST TO ME, SO I'M SURE YOU UNDERSTAND.
YES...
DRAGON KING!!
THE ONLY THING THAT CAN END THIS HUMAN'S SUFFERING IS DEATH!!
AS YOU WISH, MASTER.
NO! PLEASE DON'T!!
PLEASE DON'T KILL HIM!!

SPLAT

CHAPTER 47

!!!
RIKO!!!
WHAP
AH!
AAAH!
RIKO!!
RIKO!!
WHAT A FOOL YOU ARE...
...BRINGING A WATER SHIKI TO CONFRONT A FIRE DRAGON SUCH AS I?
And a lowly first-level Shiki at that.

IT'S YOUR FAULT THAT RIKO IS DEAD!!
UNH...
AH... AH...
DRAGON KING?
I...
NO...
I WASN'T EXILED HERE TO DO THINGS LIKE THIS!!
I...
DRAGON KING! WHAT'S WRONG?
NO!
NO, NO! I...
I...
I...

THAT'S ENOUGH, DRAGON KING!
FWUP
SWUP
WHO ARE YOU TWO?
A COUPLE OF CROWS?
WE OF THE TENGU CLAN WILL TAKE THE BOY NOW!
WE'RE THE CHIEF DISCIPLES OF SÔJÔ, THE PRIEST OF MT. KURAMA.

KOTARO!
KOJIRO!
FW
ASH
WE'RE HERE TO DO BATTLE WITH YOU!!

KRAK KRAK
FLASH
KRAK
WOO

...
HEH... I SEE.
SO THE TENGU CLAN IS WILLING TO MAKE AN ENEMY OF ME?

SŌJŌ, YOU FOOL!!

VERY WELL ...
I'LL BEGIN BY TURNING YOU TWO INTO A FOUNTAIN OF BLOOD!
TMP
WOOSH
KOTARO ...
PROTECT KUROSAKI. TAKE HIM BACK TO KURAMA AND AWAIT SŌJŌ'S ORDERS.
WHAT ABOUT YOU, KOJIRO?
I'LL STAY HERE AND BUY YOU SOME TIME.
THIS IS AN INCREDIBLE OPPORTUNITY.

RRMMM
HE'S THE GREATEST SWORDSMITH IN THE IMAGINARY WORLD...
...AND THE GREATEST SWORDSMAN.
I MAY NEVER HAVE ANOTHER CHANCE TO FACE THE ONE WHO WAS CALLED THE SACRED SWORDSMAN.
TMP
ISN'T THAT JUST LIKE YOU?
ALL RIGHT, THEN. I'LL GO BACK.
Oh, brother.
BUY US AS MUCH TIME AS YOU CAN.
BRR

AAAAAAAAAAH!!
AAAAAH!!
?!
DAMN!
DAMN!!
DAMN !!!
TMP
TMP
AAAAAH!!
RIKO!!

AAAAAAAAAH!!
AAAH!!
...SURVIVE.
BA-BUMP
DRAGON KING...
PLEASE, PLEASE...
BA-BUMP
huff

THWAP
FORGIVE ME.
I CAN'T LOSE YOU HERE.
GOOD LUCK, KOJIRO!
FWAP
HURRY UP AND GO!
YOU THINK I'LL LET YOU GET AWAY?
WOOSH

THWAK
AGH!!
DAMN!
TMP
IT'LL RIP OFF HIS WINGS AND TEAR HIS ARMS AND LEGS APART!!
HEH HEH HEH. THAT SWORD WILL FOLLOW YOUR BROTHER NO MATTER WHERE HE GOES.
KLUMP
KRAK KRAK
Heh...
YOU THINK YOUR THREATS WORRY US, DRAGON KING?

YOU THINK THAT NONSENSE IS GOING TO GET TO ME?
I WOULD'VE EXPECTED MORE FROM THE SACRED SWORDS-MAN.
NOW GET READY TO FIGHT!
TMP
NO!
I HAVE FAITH IN KOTARO.
HOW PATHETIC ...
YOU HAVE FAITH? WHAT WILL THAT GET YOU, YOU STUPID CROW?

KRAK KRAK
IN THE IMAGINARY WORLD, THE LAW OF THE JUNGLE PREVAILS!!
FAITH OR NO FAITH, THE WEAK MUST DIE!!
KRAK
I'LL WASTE NO TIME PLAYING WITH CROWS.
WHOOM
I'LL LET MY "LEFT HAND" DEAL WITH YOU.

FWAP
Hmph.
STUBBORN, ISN'T HE?
WOOSH

RRMMMBB

IT DOESN'T MATTER WHERE YOU FLEE TO, CROW!!
THE DRAGON KING ORDERED ME TO KILL YOU--AND I SHALL!!

UNLIKE YOU, I CAN NEVER GROW WEARY.
I'LL CHASE YOU UNTIL YOUR WINGS CRUMBLE AND FALL APART.
HEH HEH...
YOU'RE A NASTY LITTLE DEVIL.
I'd rather be pursued by a hot chick.
IF I WERE BY MYSELF, I MIGHT HAVE A CHANCE, BUT...
...CARRYING KUROSAKI, HE IS BOUND TO CATCH UP WITH ME SOONER OR LATER.
FWAP
I'M NOT WORRIED ABOUT MYSELF, BUT...
...I'VE GOT TO PROTECT KUROSAKI!

Topic 1: Seishi Yokomizo

If I'm not going to talk about him, then who am I going to talk about? I mean, in my opinion--or should I say, in the opinion of most Japanese people--he is a famous and respected writer. I love him. I prefer his Professor Yuri series over his Kindaichi books. And his early works are strangely beautiful. My favorite Yokomizo work is *Rental Boat No. 13*. It's so good. I really love his throat-slitting books. I also really liked *The Ghost Man* and *Walk in the Night*. *The Lightening Bug* is painfully delightful. All of his books are really interesting; I recommend them all. By the way, of the Kindaichi books, my favorite is *The Devil's Song*. It's beautiful. The way the victims are killed in Yokomizo's books is really beautiful. That's why I like him. I also like his uniquely macabre Japanese style.

The recent editions of his novels are rewritten in modern Japanese, but they're five times scarier when you read them in the original format. I'm really happy that I finally found the complete works of Seishi Yokomizo, which was released in the 49th year of the Showa period (1974). I recommend it. The cover is totally gross.

THOOM

!!

WHOOM
AAH!!
NO!
FOOL!
HUMAN!
YOUR LIFE IS MINE!

Chapter 48

UNH!

YOU'RE NAIVE, CROW!

HA HA HA HA!

HUMAN!
YOUR LIFE IS MINE!
NAMU-SAN!!
WHUP

SHOOM
AAAAH!!
GAAAH!!
BOOM
CRASH LANDING
FWAP
KURO-SAKI!!
ARE YOU ALL RIGHT?

...
KURO-SAKI...
AT THIS RATE, WE'RE BOTH GONERS!
HMM
THOOM
WOOO
THE SPIRIT OF FUTSU IS A TOUGH OPPONENT.
IT WON'T STOP ATTACK-ING UNTIL IT'S BEEN DESTROYED.
IT'S NOT A LIVING THING.
THE ONLY WAY TO ESCAPE FROM THIS DESERT IS TO TELEPORT OURSELVES TO ANOTHER DIMENSION!!

↓Yeah, he's mad.
NOOOO!!!
SHAKE
SHAKE
SHAKE
YOU DIRTY ROTTEN CROW! THAT WASN'T FAIR!
AAAH!!
AAAH!!
Futsu
SHUT UP!!
EVERY-THING'S FAIR IN WAR!!
HANG ON TIGHT...
...KURO-SAKI!!

HMPH.
WHUP
SŌJŌ...
BY THE ORDER OF THE KEEPER OF THE SUZAKU GATE...
...OPEN THE DOOR THAT LEADS FROM HERE TO ETERNITY.
RRMMMBB
GIVE ME STRENGTH!!
NOW!! OPEN THE PORTAL!!

KRAK
AAH! CAN IT BE?
KRAK
ONLY THE KEEPERS OF THE GATES OF THE FOUR GODS HOLD THE POWER TO OPEN A WORMHOLE!!
INTER-DIMENSIONAL TELEPORTA-TION?!!
DOOM

FWASH
TMP
SORYUU!
TMP
I HEARD YOU FOUND HISOKA!!

HUH?
OH, TSUZUKI.
COME IN AND I'LL EXPLAIN.
WHAT THE--
BEEP
HANYA
FWAP
THE 12 SHIKI GATHERED IN ONE PLACE...?
DID SOMETHING HAPPEN, FATHER?
HELLO, KIJIN. AND RIKUGO IS WITH YOU. GOOD.
A GRAVE EMERGENCY FACES US.

THOOM
THE FORCE FIELD SEPARATING THIS WORLD FROM THE FUYUU DESERT HAS BEEN DAMAGED!
WE HAVE TO START REPAIR-ING IT IMMEDI-ATELY!
Force field?
HOW COULD THAT HAPPEN?!
Has that dragon out-smarted us?
THE FORCE FIELD COULD NEVER HAVE BEEN TORN APART FROM THE INSIDE.

THEN HOW THE--?

...

FORGET THAT CRAP! WHAT ABOUT HISOKA?!

WHERE'S HISOKA?!

VEEN

WHAT WAS THAT, TSUZUKI?

UH...

WHAM

HOW DARE YOU?!!

WHAT ARE YOU CALLING CRAP?!!

WHAT DOES A HUMAN LIKE YOU KNOW?!!
IF THE FORCE FIELD BREAKS, THEN THAT FIEND WILL COME HERE!
AND OUR LAND WILL BE TORN APART BY WAR YET AGAIN!
WHAP
JUST WHEN WE'VE FINALLY BEGUN TO LIVE IN PEACE, WE MAY BE ABOUT TO LOSE EVERYTHING!
FATHER!!
DO YOU UNDER-STAND, TSUZUKI?!!
AH...

Topic 2: Kou Kitamori

Lately I really like his Gunchi Hatake series. The latest one is *The Laughing Mask*. (It includes the stories "Sealed Demon Meeting," "The Laughing Mask," "No Return," "The Double Shinigami," and "Evil Buddha.") It's really good. He's written a lot of stuff besides the Detective Gunchi series, but I've only read this series, so that's all I can write about.

First of all, anybody who likes folklore should read these books. I love folklore, so I really got into this series from the very beginning. Detective Gunchi is so hot...even if she is a girl. She's like, "Please forgive my corrupt, iced-coffee loving ways." I also like her unreliable assistant Mikuni. That's right, I love how the main character is a woman and her assistant is a man. That system sounds good to me (laugh). As for the story, Professor Gunchi and her assistant Mikuni solve all sorts of mysteries. The stories aren't really flashy, but it's really cool how the plots all involve folklore. "No Return" is a really dark story set in old Japan. It's actually influenced my work on this manga. I like those dark stories.

I can't wait to read "File Two."

S-SORRY... I-I DIDN'T MEAN TO...

Um...

I-I'M SORRY ...

SOB SOB

UH...

Suzaku yelling

Stop picking on Tsuzuki!

Tenko yelling

Don't you make my Tsuzuki cry!

Byakko yelling

HE'S CRYING BECAUSE YOU SHOVED THAT SCARY MUG OF YOURS IN HIS FACE.

You made him cry!

Wa ha ha

UP!!

I can't help it if my face is scary.

I'M SORRY.

Sigh

I DIDN'T MEAN TO TAKE IT OUT ON YOU.

PAT PAT

IT'S ALL MY FAULT.

DON'T CRY.

Doesn't it look like Soryuu's really on the defensive? (Ha.)

TSUZUKI, DO YOU REMEMBER KURIKARA, THE DRAGON KING?
Uh-huh.
SOMETHING HAS RIPPED THE FORCE FIELD THAT HOLDS KURIKARA IN HIS WORLD OF EXILE.
Huh?
RIPPED?
THE FUYUU DESERT IS ON ANOTHER WORLD, IN A DIMENSION FAR FROM THE IMAGINARY WORLD.
IN ORDER TO GET THERE, YOU HAVE TO USE A TELEPORTATION MACHINE IN TENKU'S CASTLE.
THAT'S RIGHT.
UNLESS A WORMHOLE JUST HAPPENS TO OPEN UP FOR YOU.
!
YOU CAN'T MEAN...
KUROSAKI WENT MISSING AT THE VERY MOMENT THAT THE DAMAGE TO THE FORCE FIELD OCCURRED.
HE ALMOST CERTAINLY FELL INTO THE FUYUU DESERT.
THAT'S WHAT HAPPENED, Ō. HERE ARE YOUR ORDERS.
KIJIN WILL ASSIST Ō.
SUZAKU AND BYAKKO WILL GUARD THE CASTLE IN CASE OF AN ATTACK.
WHAT? DON'T TELL ME YOU'RE GOING TO...

THIS IS KURIKARA WE'RE TALKING ABOUT. I HAVE TO CONFRONT HIM!

Daddy!
DON'T WORRY. I'M JUST GOING TO GO HAVE A LOOK.

GOOD LUCK.

LET'S GO, TSUZUKI!
FWIP

OKAY!!
THOOM
HANG ON, HISOKA.

I'M COMING!
FWASH
BOOM
AAAAH!!
MMBB
RK
FWAP FWAP
OOOO

...!!

HEH HEH HEH! YOU REALLY ARE AS STUPID AS A BIRD.

BOOM

ACCIDENTS LIKE THIS CAN EASILY HAPPEN WHEN YOU'RE MOVING THROUGH DIMENSIONS!

HEH HEH HEH! HA HA HA! I HAVE TO THANK YOU, CROW!!
IT WAS NICE OF YOU TO FREE ME FROM THAT BLOODY DESERT!!
RRMMMMBB
FUTSU?!
IT CAN'T BE.
I'LL TURN THIS LAND INTO A SEA OF FIRE AGAIN! HA HA HA!
HA HA HA HA!
THE CENTURIES HAVE DONE NOTHING TO COOL MY HATRED!!
LOOK OUT, 12 SHIKI! LOOK OUT, EMPEROR!

CHAPTER 49

FWASH
WOOOOO

I'VE FINALLY ESCAPED FROM THAT BLOODY DESERT!!
HA HA HA HA!! I DID IT!!

WAR!! THIS IS WAR!!
I'LL COVER THIS LAND IN FLAME AND DESTROY THOSE WRETCHED 12 SHIKI!
THE DRAGON KING WILL RULE THE IMAGINARY WORLD!!
WA HA HA HA!!
HA HA HA!!
GRR...
WHAT THE HELL?!
I CAN'T BELIEVE I HELPED FREE THAT WAR CRIMINAL!
WOOSH
I'VE NO TIME TO PLAY WITH CROWS!
I'VE GOT TO START FIGHTING BEFORE THE DRAGON KING ARRIVES!!
I CAN'T ALLOW IT TO REMAIN FREE.
VWOOM
WAIT!!
?!

BOOM
!!!

HMPH... WHAT IS IT, CROW? I'M IN A HURRY!

Oops

I HAVE IMPORTANT MATTERS TO ATTEND TO.

RUN BACK TO THAT PRIEST WITH YOUR TAIL BETWEEN YOUR LEGS AND TELL HIM WHAT YOU'VE DONE!

SHUT UP!!

Blah, blah, blah... You really piss me off!

KURO-SAKI...
Unh
..HANG ON A LITTLE LONGER.
THE DRAGON KING'S POWER IS CONSUMING HIM!!
I'VE GOT TO HURRY!!

I HAVE NO IDEA...
...WHAT HAPPENED BETWEEN KURIKARA AND SORYUU IN THE PAST.
THAT WAS LONG BEFORE I WAS BORN.
BUT THE VILLAGE ELDERS AND THE PRIEST OFTEN TOLD ME THE STORIES.
THE OCEAN DRIED UP AND THE LAND WAS CONTAMINATED.
MANY OF OUR FRIENDS WERE INCINERATED BY KURIKARA'S FIERY BLASTS.
THEY SAY IT WAS THE VERY IMAGE OF HELL!!

FWASH

I'LL NEVER LET THAT HAPPEN AGAIN!!!

IT'S A KOTARO ORIGINAL!!
VWMM
GET READY FOR THE SEVEN LEAGUES FORCE FIELD SPELL!!
WHAT THE HELL ARE YOU UP TO, CROW?!
ARE YOU TRYING TO SEAL ME IN HERE?!
FOOL! AS IF YOU COULD!
WHAT?!
NOW TO GET RID OF YOU ONCE AND FOR ALL!!!
I SUMMON THE GREATEST POWER OF THE GODS!!

THUNDER KING!!
COME FORTH !!!

THOOM
KRAK
KRAK
KRAK
KRAK
KRAK
KRAK
thoom

KA-BOOSH

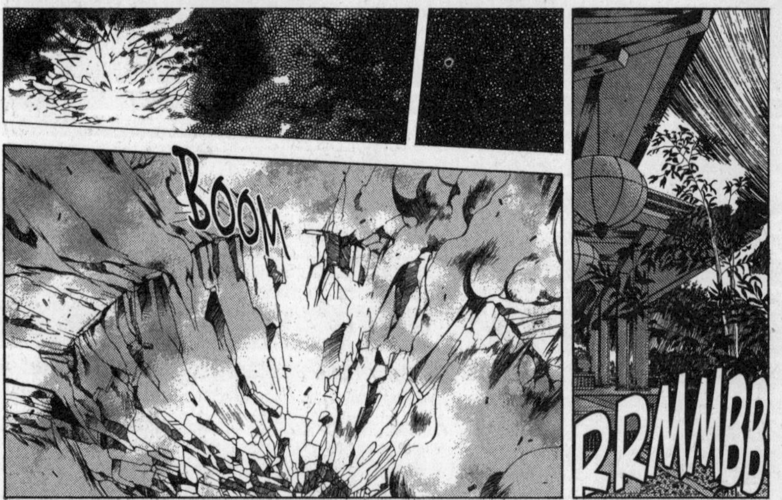

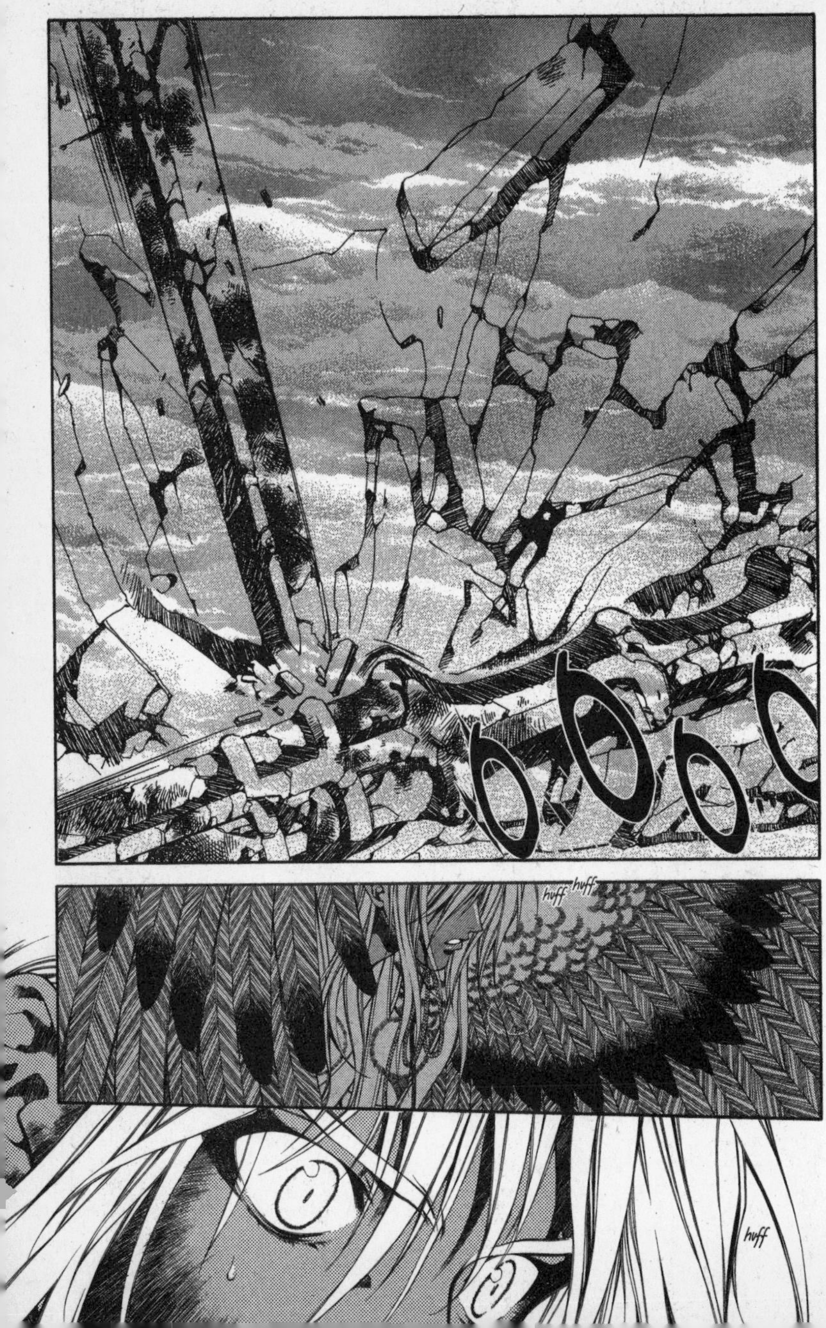

huff huff

WOOO
IT'S OVER.
BUT THERE'S NOT MUCH LEFT IN ME, EITHER.

Tired

THE POWER OF MT. KURAMA, WHICH I SPENT HUNDREDS OF YEARS ACCUMULATING IN MY BODY...

HUFF... HUFF...

...IS COMPLETELY GONE.

NOT BAD FOR A CROW...

...EH, FUTSU?!

DAMN...

HOW AM I GOING TO EXPLAIN THIS ONE?

exhausted

I GUESS I'D BETTER HEAD BACK TO THE TEMPLE.

WOBBLE

WOBBLE

WOBBLE

...SPIRIT OF FUTSU...

I CAN'T BELIEVE THOSE STUPID CROWS WANDERED OVER HERE.
I SHOT ONE OF THEM DOWN.
CROWS?
WHAT THE ...?!!
YOU'D BETTER NOT HAVE DONE ANYTHING TO THE GATE KEEPERS!!
CALM DOWN, TSUZUKI.

RRMMBB
THOOM
LONG TIME NO SEE.

THOOM
YOU'RE STILL ALIVE, EH, KURIKARA?

UNFORTUNATELY FOR YOU.

...

AND...

...YOUR HAIR HAS GROWN.

BRAGGING

You like?! Isn't it shiny and silky?!

HMPH

POW
WHAK
SORYUU, YOU MORON! WHY ARE YOU TALKING ABOUT STUPID STUFF?
SPIRITUAL POWER RESIDES IN THE HAIR.

HAIR IS A DRAGON'S SOURCE OF POWER. DRAGONS JUDGE EACH OTHER BY THE LENGTH OF THEIR HAIR.

THE LONGER THE HAIR IS, THE OLDER AND MORE FORMIDABLE THE DRAGON.

So many visitors today...
I haven't had a moment to myself.

Yeah, and your house was destroyed.

YOU FIEND!

HOW MUCH HAS YOUR POWER INCREASED IN EXILE, KURIKARA?
HAH!
Half of his room managed to survive the battle.
...
WHAT...?
KURIKARA! WHAT HAVE YOU DONE WITH HISOKA?!
HISOKA?
OH, YOU MEAN THE BOY?

I DON'T KNOW.
LAST I SAW, ONE OF THOSE CROWS WAS CARRYING HIM AWAY.
YANK
I GAVE HIM A BLAST OF MY POWER, SO HE MAY BE DEAD BY NOW.
WHAT ?!!
WE MUST'VE JUST MISSED HIM.

LET'S GO HOME, TSUZUKI.
SORYUU!!
HEY!
BUT...

I'VE GOT A BAD FEELING ABOUT THIS.

Topic 3: Ellery Queen

I love these books. I really love them. Different translators write the name differently (laugh). (I'm not sure whether it's Ellery or Ellerii. Sometimes there's a space between Ellery and Queen, and sometimes there isn't. I like that too.) The first book I read wasn't part of the famous Countries series. It was the book *The Tragedy of Y*, and the main character was the actor Drury Lane. (The X, Y, Z series is published under the penname Barnaby Ross, so I didn't even know it was an Ellery Queen novel at first. Duh.) I read X and Z too, but *The Tragedy of Y* is my favorite. I read it back in grade school, but considering that it's really easy to read and written for kids, it was actually pretty scary (laugh). The old woman who gets killed is really creepy. I was shocked when I found out who the killer was. Anyway, I've always liked Ellery Queen. Ellery Queen is often compared to Agatha Christie, but I can't stand Christie's books. Maybe that's unusual.

I LOVE THE CLASSICS!

If a mystery novel doesn't have a detective solving the mystery, then I just can't accept it. I won't accept it. I think people who like Conan Doyle will like these books as well.

I DON'T SEE THE SPIRIT OF FUTSU...

...KURIKARA'S RIGHT HAND!

HUH?

I HOPE MY HUNCH IS WRONG.

WAIT JUST A MOMENT.

ARE WE NOT ARCH-ENEMIES?

ISN'T THIS OUR TEARFUL REUNION?

WE HAVE A LOT OF CATCHING UP TO DO.
DON'T WE?
Shake
Shake
Shake
SORYUU...
SHAKE
SHAKE
SHAKE

SEMOLINA FLOUR
CIRIO
OLIVE OIL
TRADITIONAL TASTE
Rubino
CRESP
FOOD LOVER
ha ha ha ha
Munch Munch
How 'bout a drink?
CHAPTER 50

WOOO
CATCHING UP?

RIDICULOUS!
I HAVE NOTHING TO SAY TO YOU!
HEH
YOU'RE STILL A TOUGH COOKIE.
And narrow-minded.
He should add stubborn as well.
SHUT UP.
←Daddy

WAIT A MINUTE.
I THOUGHT YOU WERE BUSY TRYING TO STOP THE WORM-HOLES.
COME ON, TSUZUKI. WE'RE LEAVING.
WHAP
IGNORING
WHOOM
WE CAN'T BE AWAY FROM THE CASTLE ANY LONGER!!
SORYUU!!
WAAH!
DON'T YOU THINK IT'S RATHER ODD...

WHY DOESN'T THE EMPEROR SAVE THE IMAGINARY WORLD?
WITH HIS POWERS, IT WOULD BE EASY.
THE ELECTRICITY CREATED BY HUMAN CIVILIZATION IS SHINING LIGHT UPON THE DARKNESS WHERE WE HIDE, AND ROBBING US OF OUR HOMES.
THAT'S ONE THING.
BUT THIS TRULY COULD BE THE END OF THE IMAGINARY WORLD.
SHIVERS
SHUT UP.
...
LISTEN, SORYUU.
HAVE YOU EVER EVEN SEEN THE EMPEROR?

HAVE YOU EVER ACTUALLY HEARD HIS VOICE?
SHUT UP!
HAVE YOU EVER FELT THE WARMTH ...
WOO
...OF HIS LIVING BODY, SORYUU?
SOR-YUU!
STOP IT!
BOTH OF YOU!!
I MEAN...
THOOM
...DOES THIS SO-CALLED EMPEROR EVEN EXIST?
SPLASH
Assuming battle stance

SORYUU!! NO!!!
WHA ...?

WHAT'S YOUR GAME, HUMAN?
YOU'VE REALIZED THAT YOU CAN'T DEFEAT ME AND YOU WANT TO INGRATIATE YOURSELF WITH ME, EH?
NOT AT ALL.
I HAVE A QUESTION FOR YOU, KURIKARA ...
WHY DID YOU START THAT WAR?
FROM WHAT I'VE HEARD...
...IT DOESN'T SEEM LIKE YOU WANTED TO DESTROY THE IMAGINARY WORLD.
DID YOU HAVE ...
...SOME OTHER MOTIVE?
TMP

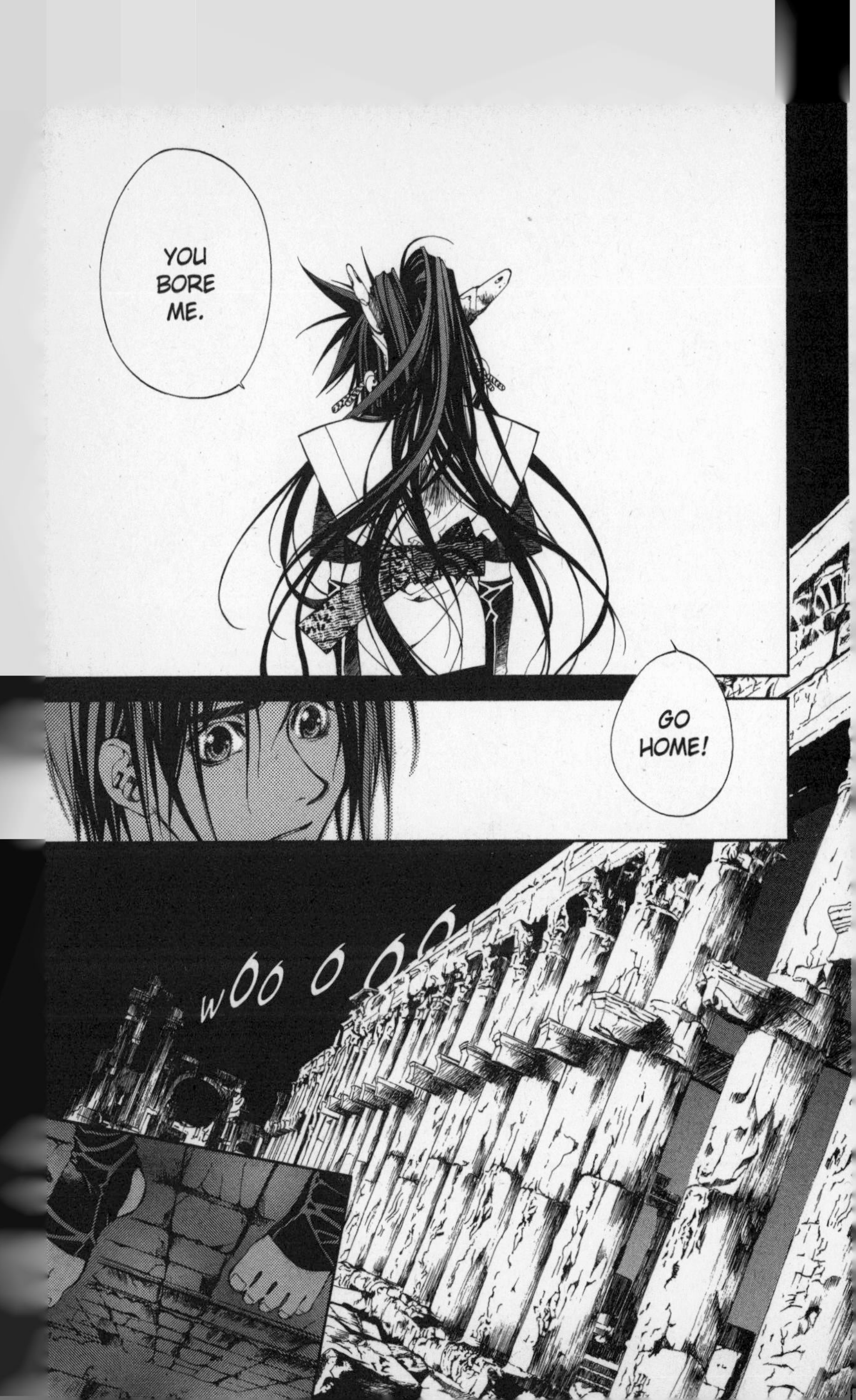
GO HOME!
YOU BORE ME.
WOOOOOO

HMM...
EVEN IN THIS BARREN PLACE, A FLOWER BLOOMS.
SNIK
...
WHY DID YOU START THE WAR?
WITH-OUT A CAUSE...
...WORTH FIGHTING FOR...

...NO ONE WOULD EVER GO TO WAR.
THEY CAN EXILE ME TO THE RUINS OF THIS GOD-FORSAKEN FORMER CAPITAL...
...AND BLAME ME IF THEY WISH, BUT...
WOOO

WOOO
!!
WOOOOO

I WILL NEVER STOP FIGHTING FOR JUSTICE.

REEEN
REEEN
REEEN

WELL THEN, WATARI ...
I'LL BE ON MY WAY.
CHING
Kamakura
(the Kurosaki Residence)
HUH?
sleepy

POP
KREK
KREK
KRK
KRK
KRK
KRAK
SNAP
yawn
KRAK

↑ His posture is bad so his joints crack a lot.

SKRITCH SKRITCH
Alarm Clock

WAH!!
WHAT? IT'S ONLY SEVEN?!
I WAS UP ALL NIGHT READING MEDICAL BOOKS!
This bites!
REE
REE
YOU'RE WASTING DAY-LIGHT.
He gets up at five.
NOW MAKE YOURSELF PRESENT-ABLE BEFORE MIYA COMES IN WITH BREAKFAST.
REE
I don't care if it is someone else's house, it's a waste of electricity to study at night! Do it in the daytime!
CONSERVE RESOURCES

ALL RIGHT, I'M OFF TO INVESTIGATE THE RUINS OF THE SCHOOL.

AND BE CAREFUL WHAT YOU SAY. YOU MUSTN'T LET ANYONE DISCOVER THAT YOU'RE A--
Got it?
YACK YACK YACK YACK
FWIP
HUH? HUH?
THE RUINS OF THE SCHOOL?
WHOA! WAIT, TATSUMI!!

Topic 4: Arisu Arisukawa

As a fan of Queen, I can't leave out this author (laugh). Let's talk about Arisu Arisukawa I guess it's kind of weird for a guy to be so into *Alice in Wonderland*, but let's put that aside. He writes classical style mystery stories. As a lover of classic mysteries, I can't get enough of him. When am I going to try something new (laugh)?

♚

I've only read the Himura series, so I can't really talk about anything else. The Himura mysteries really draw me in (laugh). Himura's past is pretty mysterious, but in *A Study in Scarlet* we find out a little. Hmm... I can't wait the sequel. But then, I'm always late, so I can't complain about other authors (laugh). I probably could never be friends with Detective Himura because he's a cat lover—I'm allergic. By the way, what first got me into the series was the scene in *The Loon's Seduction* where the detective puts his friend's copy of *Alice in Wonderland* back on the bookshelf upside down!

Detective Himura ♥ is so cool.

WHAT? YOU'RE REALLY GOING TO THAT OLD SCHOOL?
I thought you were joking.
WHY SHOULDN'T I?
WELL, I DON'T KNOW...

BUT REMEMBER WHAT HISOKA'S FATHER SAID.
RUI'S FILE WAS STOLEN.
HE WAS VERY GOOD, BUT A MONTH AGO HE DIED IN AN ACCIDENT.

THE POLICE HAVE ALREADY SEARCHED THE SCHOOL.
I DOUBT THAT YOU'LL FIND ANYTHING THERE.
WOULDN'T YOU BE BETTER OFF INVESTIGATING SOMETHING ELSE?
Since you've got a tech wizard like me with you...
...we should hack the police department's computers or something.

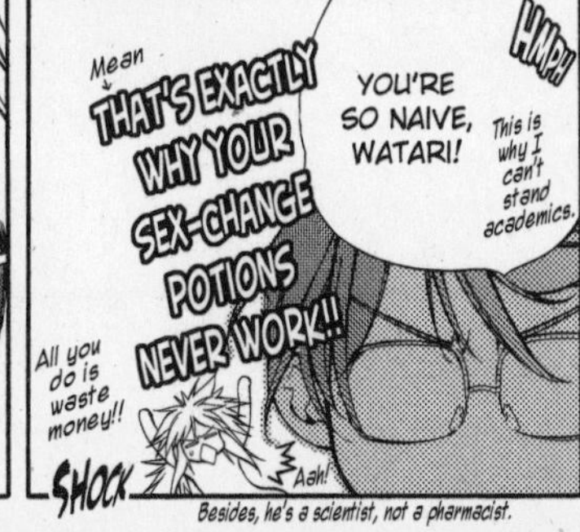

HMPH
YOU'RE SO NAIVE, WATARI!
This is why I can't stand academics.
Mean
THAT'S EXACTLY WHY YOUR SEX-CHANGE POTIONS NEVER WORK!!
All you do is waste money!!
SHOCK
Aah!

NOW LISTEN...

Besides, he's a scientist, not a pharmacist.

NAGARE INSISTED THAT DOCTOR HAZAMA'S DEATH WAS AN ACCIDENT, SO...

...WE CAN DEDUCE THAT THE LOCAL POLICE COOPERATED WITH THE KUROSAKI FAMILY.

NAGARE PROBABLY ASKED THE CHIEF OF POLICE TO RULE DR. HAZAMA'S DEATH AN ACCIDENT TO CLOSE THE INVESTIGATION.

IF THE DOCTOR WAS MURDERED, BUT IT WAS MADE TO LOOK ACCIDENTAL...

...THEY MAY HAVE OVER-LOOKED THINGS.
※ The Doctor's death was attributed to a fall.

There you go.

OF COURSE. SO THAT MEANS...

Yes.

THERE MAY STILL BE UNDISCOVERED EVIDENCE IN THE SCHOOL.
Small town police are notoriously sloppy.

↖ Stereotype

IT WON'T TAKE LONG.
I'M JUST GOING TO GIVE THE SCHOOL A QUICK ONCE-OVER.
I DON'T KNOW...
REE REE
I CAN'T REST UNLESS I SEE IT FOR MYSELF.
BESIDES...
REE
REE
...WE HAVE TO BE THOROUGH FOR HISOKA'S SAKE.
WOW... YOU REALLY DO CARE ABOUT KIDS AND CLOSE FRIENDS, HUH, TATSUMI?
SKRITCH
SKRITCH
REE
I'LL BE BACK IN AN HOUR.
REE
REE
OKAY.
I'LL CHECK OUT WHAT I CAN AROUND HERE.
THANK YOU.

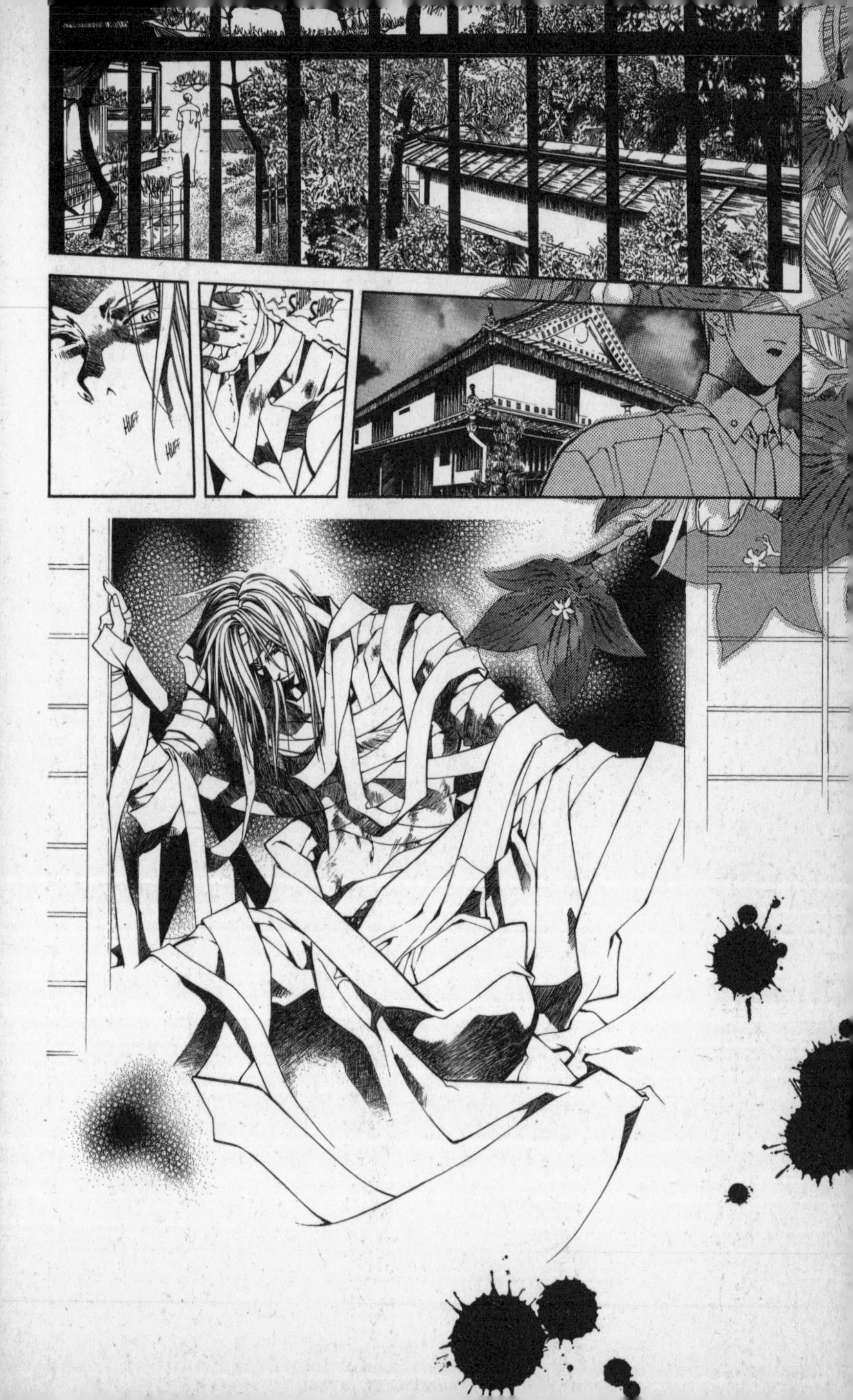
SHIVER SHIVER
HUFF
HUFF

CHAPTER 51

WOOOO

THOOM

DOOM

THERE!

WHAT IS IT?

A PICTURE?

KREEK
I CAN'T REALLY TRUST ANYONE BUT MYSELF.
KREEK
KREEK
IT'S NOT THAT I HAVE AN EXALTED IDEA OF MY OWN ABILITIES.
...
IN MY DAY, THAT WAS THE ONLY WAY TO SURVIVE.
YOU CAN'T RELY ON YOUR GOVERN-MENT OR ON OTHER PEOPLE.
IF THE KUROSAKI FAMILY HAS THE POLICE UNDER ITS CONTROL...
...THEN WE'D BETTER TREAD SOFTLY.
SMILE
HEH
KREEK
KREEK

HE DID MEDICAL RESEARCH HERE.
I CAN STILL SENSE DOCTOR HAZAMA'S PRESENCE.
WOOO
THOOM
WOOO
SHWOOO
WOOO
THERE IT IS!!

SHOWA YEAR 53... THAT WAS 1978.
Pretty old.

NO WONDER THE INVESTI-GATORS MISSED IT.

WHUP
TUP
SWUFF

?!!
DOOM

WHAT THE...?
IT CAN'T BE...
REE
REE
THEN THIS MEANS ...
REE
REE
REE

THERE WERE TWO OF THEM?!!
MASTER ...

MIYA?
WHAT IS IT?
THERE'S SOME-THING I WANT TO ASK YOU.
MAY I?
I'M BACK.

I'll use this opportunity to talk about the anime.

It'd be a shame not to mention it, after all. The anime...yeah, the anime. It's amazing. The characters move! Every artist dreams of having his or her work made into anime. And it's all thanks to your support. Thank you very much!

♛

It started out as 26 episodes, but they ended up shortening it by half. It's going to be a very concentrated 13 episodes. Anyway, the voice actors are so gorgeous, it brings tears to my eyes. That alone is enough to satisfy my hunger. Kazuhiko Inoue plays Oriya. That's more than I could have hoped for. (I just wish he had more lines.) And the opening is really exciing. I mean, it's almost a show in itself (laugh). As for the actual show, they have a limited amount of time and episodes, so they had to cut a lot. Making anime is really tough. Seriously. It costs a lot of money. *No joke.*

♛

Actually, I went to the recording session of the first episode, and afterwards I had the amazing experience of going out with Shinichiro Miki who plays Tsuzuki. Sorry I'm such a dull conversationalist, Miki-san.

But please cut back on the sake--for your health.

TATSUMI !!
BLAB BLAB
Hm.
YOU CAME BACK AT THE PERFECT TIME!
JUST WHAT I'D EXPECT FROM MY ASSISTANT!!
YOU'RE IT!
YOU CAN TAKE OVER NOW.
WHAT ?!
WAH!!
THEN YOU'LL COME WITH ME, TATSUMI?
GASP
HUH ?!!

YACK
YACK
WHAT ?
WHAT ?
WHAT ?
YACK
WHAT IS GOING ON?!!
SKRUNCH
I KNEW IT. THE MASTER'S CLOTHES ARE JUST HIS SIZE. ♥
I haven't lost my touch.
DON'T YOU LIKE THIS DESIGN?
It's very sexy.
NO! I LIKE THIS ONE.
you have bad taste.
WHAT ABOUT THIS OBI?
Do you think this fan will go with the yukata?
OH, THAT'S LOVELY!
Lots of personality.
THUMP
KRASH
AAAAH!!!
WHAM
THUD
Pretending he's busy
FORGIVE ME, TATSUMI. I'M IN THE MIDDLE OF SOMETHING VERY IMPORTANT.
He's speaking standard Japanese for some reason.

BOOM BOOM
BOOM
OH.
MEN WHO LOOK GOOD IN A KIMONO ARE SUCH A TURN-ON.
SIGH

...
THANK YOU.
Well...
I ADMIT I WAS A BIT TAKEN ABACK WHEN YOU SUDDENLY STARTED SHOVING ME INTO A YUKATA.
Naturally.
YACK
YACK
Oh! ♥ You're blush-ing. ♥
HEH HEH... I'M SORRY.
I JUST REALLY WANTED TO INVITE YOU TWO TO ENJOY THE SUMMER FESTIVAL IN YUKATAS.
Too bad the Doctor has to work.
BY THE WAY, WHOSE YAKUTA IS THIS?
BOOM BOOM
You're wearing your own, I pre-sume...
IT'S THE MASTER'S.
Yes, it's mine.
It's hot.
FWUP FWUP

IF YOU GO TO A JAPANESE SUMMER FESTIVAL, YOU HAVE TO WEAR A YUKATA!!

PLEASE, MASTER!

LET US BORROW A YUKATA.

Okay, but...

...

Just make sure you get all your work done.

MEMBERS OF THE "WE WANT TO SEE YOUNG GUYS IN YUKATA" CLUB.

INSISTING!

...

Sigh

DIZZY

HIS FAMILY WAS RESPECTABLE, BUT POOR.

I guess you've got to have a certain amount of pluck to work for a famous old family.

By the way, they decided who would be Tatsumi's escort by lottery.
I WON!
WINNER
AAAAAAA
AH!!! BOO HOO
Are you really servants to a noble family?
↑Going crazy
BOOM BOOM
BA-BOOM
HERE YOU GO.
Candy apple
Thanks.
BY THE WAY, MIYA ...

RATTLE
THIS MORNING I WENT TO THE OLD SCHOOL.
WIP
AND I FOUND THIS.
GASP
WHA... WHAT?
BOOM
BOOM
RATTLE
I WANTED TO GET YOUR CONFIRMATION.
THE WOMAN IN THIS PICTURE IS THE WOMAN IN THE BASEMENT, CORRECT?

IT'S RUI, ISN'T IT?!
...
YES.
THAT'S THE MISTRESS.
THEY HAVE THE SAME FACE.
THEN THEY MUST BE IDENTICAL TWINS.
MIYA...
BOOM BOOM BOOM
KLANG
WE WERE SENT TO THE KUROSAKI RESIDENCE WITHOUT ANY INFORMATION.
WE WANT TO DO ALL WE CAN FOR OUR PATIENT.
KLANG
SO PLEASE TELL ME THE TRUTH.

BOOM
IS THAT REALLY RUI?
...
I HOPE IT'S NOT THE CASE, BUT...
BA-BOOM
...HAVE WE BEEN DECEIVED?
BOOM

KAGOME, KAGOME

WHEN WILL THE BIRD COME OUT OF ITS CAGE?

THE CRANE AND THE TURTLE SLIPPED OUT AT DAWN. WHO'S THAT BEHIND YOU?

Chapter 52

BA-BOOM!
IS THE WOMAN IN THE BASEMENT REALLY RUI?
BOOM BOOM BOOM
HAVE WE BEEN DECEIVED?
MIYA!
BOOM

OH!
IS THAT YOU, MIYA?
BOOM
BOOM
AH! MR. MAYOR.
And some villagers.
ARE YOU ENJOYING THE FESTIVAL?
IT'S THE BIGGEST FESTIVAL OF THE YEAR FOR US.
YOU SHOULD LET LOOSE AND HAVE FUN, MIYA.
Oh, I see you have a gentleman friend. Ha ha ha.
It's not like that.
OKAY!
Oh...
ALLOW ME TO INTRODUCE YOU, MR. MAYOR.
THIS IS TATSUMI. HE'S HERE TO HELP CARE FOR THE MISTRESS.
HOW DO YOU DO?
SALESMAN'S SMILE
OH, OH...
SO YOU'RE DR. HAZAMA'S REPLACEMENT.
TATSUMI, THIS IS OUR MAYOR.
SHAKE
SHAKE

THANK YOU.
SO GOOD OF YOU TO COME ALL THE WAY OUT TO THE COUNTRY.
PLEASE TAKE GOOD CARE OF THE MASTER AND HIS WIFE.
THERE ARE NO DOCTORS IN THIS VILLAGE.
YOU'RE OUR ONLY HOPE, DOCTOR!
NO.
I'M JUST AN ASSISTANT.
HRMPH
TWITCH TWITCH
BEGGING EYES
WHO CARES?!
THAT MAKES NO DIFFERENCE TO US! WE WELCOME ANY-ONE WHO TRIES TO HELP THE KUROSAKI FAMILY!!
HA HA!
THANK YOU!
THANK YOU!
...All right.
THANK YOU!
THEIR HEIR, HISOKA, DIED VERY YOUNG.
THIS COULD MEAN THE END OF THE KUROSAKI LINEAGE.
THAT IS A THING...
...WE CANNOT ALLOW... FOR THE SAKE OF THE VILLAGE!!!
?!

SORRY...
SUCH AN UN-PLEASANT TOPIC.
THE DANCING WILL CONTINUE UNTIL MORNING.
PLEASE STAY AND ENJOY YOURSELF.
I MUST EXCUSE MYSELF NOW.
KLIK KLIK
...
WHAT DID HE JUST SAY?
FOR THE SAKE OF THE VILLAGE?
THE ANCESTOR OF THE KUROSAKI FAMILY WAS A HERO WHO SAVED THIS VILLAGE LONG AGO.

A HERO?
LONG AGO, A HORNED SNAKE DEMON NAMED YATONOKAMI LIVED HERE.
HIS HORNS HAD THE POWER TO BRING DISEASE AND DROUGHT. THE PEOPLE SUFFERED TERRIBLY.
EVERY SUMMER, THE PEOPLE WOULD BRING YATONOKAMI A SACRIFICE TO BE DROWNED IN THE MARSH.
NONE DARED TO DISOBEY THE GOD...
...EXCEPT ONE MAN-- THE FIRST KUROSAKI.
HIS NAME WAS REN.

BOOM
BOOM
AS THE CHIEF SAMURAI OF THE VILLAGE, REN CON-FRONTED YATONOKAMI ALL BY HIMSELF.
BOOM
HE WANTED TO FREE THE VILLAGERS FROM THE TERRORS OF DEATH, DISEASE, AND STARVATION.
AND TO THIS DAY THE KUROSAKI ARE REVERED AS A FAMILY OF HEROES.
OF COURSE...
THAT'S WHY THEY HAVE SO MUCH INFLUENCE HERE.
EVERYONE HERE, INCLUDING THE POLICE, OBEYS THE KUROSAKI.
EVEN SO, THE MAYOR'S ATTITUDE SEEMED A BIT PECULIAR.
Hmm
STILL...
AFTER A DEATH MATCH LASTING SEVEN DAYS AND NIGHTS...
...REN DEFEATED YATONOKAMI ON THE MORNING OF THE 8TH DAY.

BUT, UNLIKE THE BUDDHA, YATONOKAMI DAMNED HIS FOE!!
IT PUT A CURSE ON REN AND ALL HIS SEED.
EVEN NOW, CENTURIES LATER, THE KUROSAKI ALL DIE YOUNG IN STRANGE ACCIDENTS, OR FROM MYSTERIOUS DISEASES.
THERE ARE THOSE WHO SAY THAT IT WAS YATONOKAMI'S CURSE THAT CAUSED HISOKA'S DEATH.
YATONO-KAMI'S FIENDISH GRUDGE...
...STILL TAINTS THE BLOOD OF THE KUROSAKI.
...
Miya?
TAT-SUMI...
I CAN'T ANSWER YOUR QUESTION ABOUT THAT PHOTO.
YATONO-KAMI'S CURSE AFFECTS ALL WHO ARE CONNECTED WITH THE KUROSAKI.
PLEASE DON'T PURSUE THIS ANY FURTHER.
IT'S TRUE THAT REN WAS A HERO WHO SAVED THE VILLAGE, BUT...
AT THE SAME TIME...

...THE KUROSAKI FAMILY COMMITTED THE SIN OF KILLING A GOD.

HAAH
THEY ARE AN ACCURSED LINEAGE!!

AHH...
COUNTRY EVENINGS ARE SO PEACEFUL.
SO QUIET.
WITH NO CITY LIGHTS, YOU CAN SEE EVERY STAR.
I HAVE TO GO AND GREE PEOPLE ON BEHAL OF THE MASTER.
SMILE
FORGIVE ME BUT I'LL HAVE TO LEAVE YOU NOW.
Well...
DEALING WITH COUNTRY PEOPLE CAN BE A PAIN.
...
CURSED FOR KILLING A GOD.
HMM...

HE SACRIFICED HIMSELF TO SAVE THE VILLAGE.
AND NOW THE WHOLE FAMILY IS CURSED FOR HAVING SLAIN A GOD.
YOU MIGHT FIND SIMILAR TALES IN MANY SMALL VILLAGES THROUGH-OUT JAPAN.
Like the giant snake that King Susano fought.
BUT THERE'S SOMETHING FISHY ABOUT THIS.
RIBBIT
CURSES ARE USUALLY CAUSED BY THE RESENT-MENTS OF MORTALS.
AND IN THE OLD DAYS, BECAUSE OF POOR NUTRI-TION, PEOPLE DIDN'T LIVE LONG ANYWAY.
SIGH
IN HISOKA'S CASE, AT LEAST, HIS DEATH WAS THE DEED OF A HUMAN, NOT A GOD.
That bastard Muraki.
Maybe it's like the placebo effect.
I HAVE A HUNCH THAT THERE'S A SIDE TO THIS FAMILY THAT'S NOT SO HEROIC.
EH?
WHAT'S THAT LIGHT?
SHEEN
KRUNCH KRUNCH
!!
WOOO

Wooo

I'VE NEVER SEEN SO MANY OF THEM.
FIREFLIES...
THEY'RE BEAUTI-FUL.
Ahh
WMM
flit
WMM
WMM

IT REMINDS ME OF WHEN I WAS A BOY.
WMM
I'D CATCH THEM IN A BUG CAGE AND RELEASE THEM IN MY HOUSE.
BUT THE NEXT MORNING, THEY'D ALWAYS BE...
MY MOTHER USED TO SCOLD ME FOR BEING CRUEL.
IT'S TRUE.
THE MOON-LIGHT...
THERE'S SOME-THING IN THIS DREAM-LIKE LAND-SCAPE...
...THAT MAKES ONE BELIEVE THE OLD LEGENDS.
SUCH THINGS ARE MOST BEAUTIFUL WHEN LEFT IN THEIR OWN WORLD.
PLUP PLUP

?!!
WHAT?!
splash
splash
splash
GLUP
GACK
-GARE...
...
KOFF
KOFF

YOU FINALLY ...CAME FOR ME...

KOFF KOFF

NAGARE ...

HACK

I'M SO...HAPPY...

I MADE IT...
ACK
SWUP
...FOR YOU.
KOFF
NAGARE ...
WHAT THE...
RUI?!

CHAPTER 53

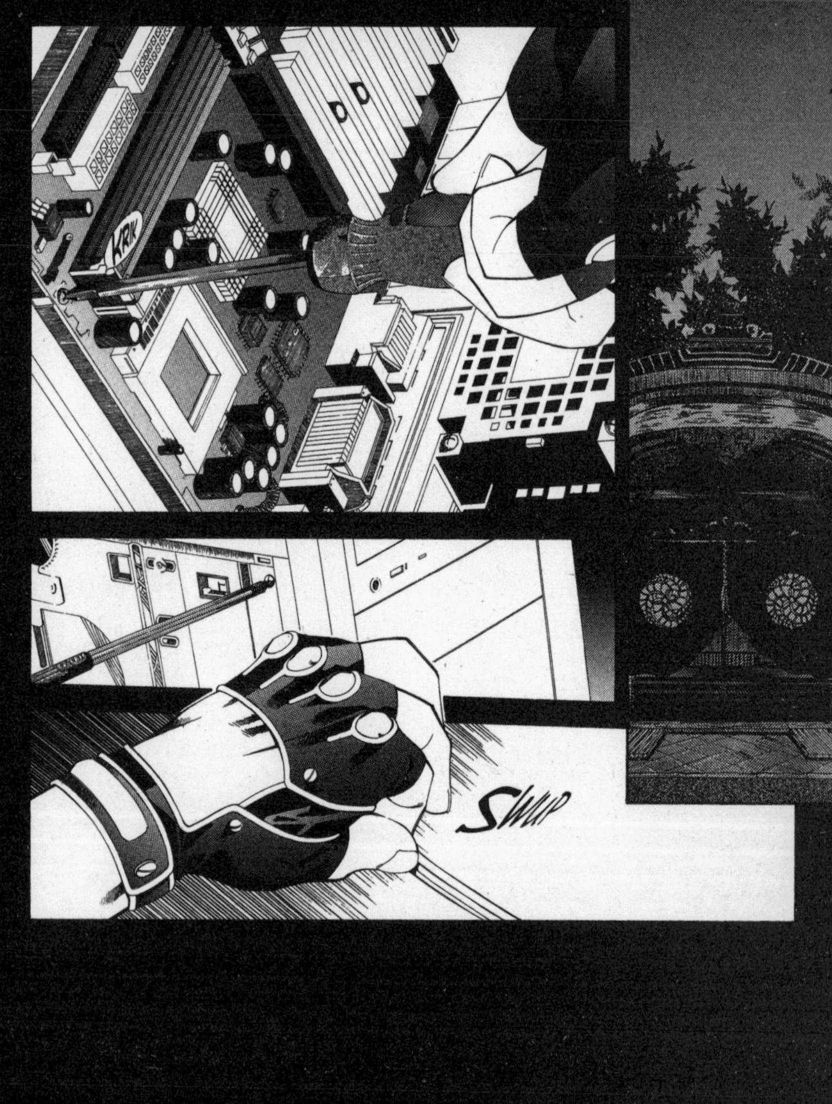
KRIK
SWIP

Hmm...

KLAK KLAK

...

KLIK

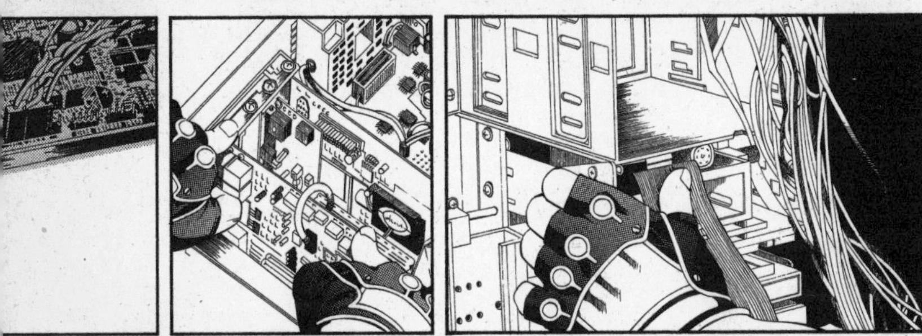

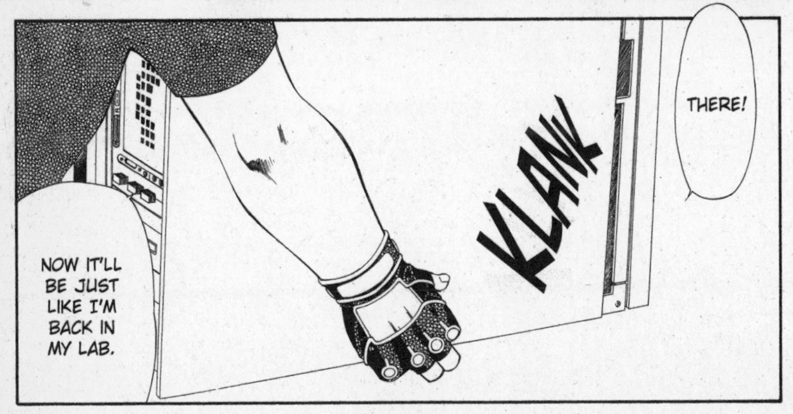

THERE!
KLANK
NOW IT'LL BE JUST LIKE I'M BACK IN MY LAB.

KLAK
KLAK KLAK
I'LL JUST SET UP THE INTERFACE...
AND CHECK THE VOLTAGE.

Enter Password
BEEP

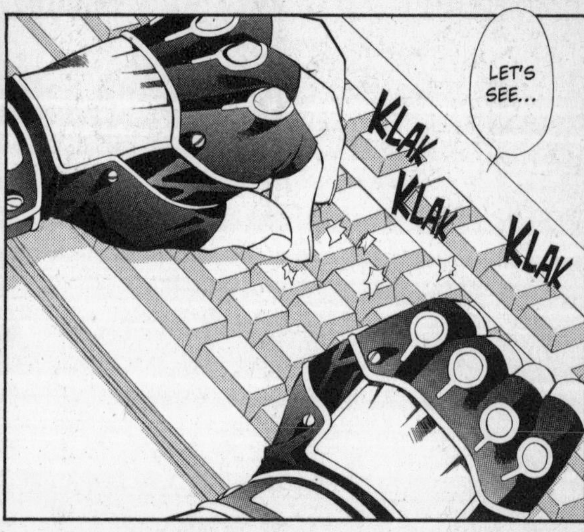
LET'S SEE...
KLAK KLAK KLAK

HMM...
THE SYSTEM MUST BE LOCKED.
SKRUFF
THIS LOOKS LIKE A TOUGH ONE.
TATSUMI SURE IS LATE.
HOW FAR AWAY WAS THAT FESTIVAL?
I was hoping to put him to work when he got back.
Don't be mean.
HUFF
SKRUSH
HUFF
UNGH...
KOFF KOFF!!

UNH
UNH
TWITCH
THUD
SHAKE SHAKE
HEH HEH HEH... SO BEAUTIFUL...
GAAH!!
UNH

Unh...
I'D LIKE TO BITE RIGHT THROUGH THAT PALE THROAT OF YOURS.
SKWEEK
HEH HEH HEH... HOW LOVELY.
WHAT A BEAUTIFUL BODY YOU HAVE, NAGARE.
Huff...
Unh...
SKWEEK
THAT MAN'S FILTHY, VILE BLOOD...
...RUNS BENEATH YOUR IVORY SKIN.
UNH...
AH...
AAAH!!
AAAH
SHIVER
AAH

YOU'RE MY PUPPET NOW. YOU'LL DO WHATEVER I SAY! HEH HEH HEH...
WA HA HA!
AAAA-AAAAAH!
AAH!
OH...
TWITCH
SHAKE
SHAKE SHAKE
UNH...
AH...
SCREAM! SUFFER!!
I WANT TO HEAR YOU BEG FOR FORGIVE-NESS!!!
YOU CAN'T RUN AWAY FROM THAT BLOOD OF YOURS!!
SWIP SWIP
UNH... AGH...
AH!
KOFF KOFF KOFF
KOFF
UNH...
PLIP PLIP
SPLAKK

NOW IT'S YOUR TURN TO SUFFER!
UGAAAAH!!!
TUP

THUMP
FLINCH
AAAAH!!!
TATSUMI?!!
WHAT'RE YOU DOING OUT THERE?!
MAY I PLEASE COME INSIDE?
DING
HERE
AAH!
A MONSTER! WAAH! NO! IT'S HORRIBLE!!
AAAAH! AAAAH!
TONK TONK TONK
He's supposed to be a man of science.
—RI!
WATARI!
IT'S ME! TATSUMI!!
TONK TONK TONK

TICK
TICK
TICK
TICK
BONG
SKWISH SKWISH
SKWISH
BONG
DID RUI'S GHOST ATTACK YOU?
BONG
NO...
IT WAS PROBABLY HER TWIN.
SHE MUST HAVE MISTAKEN ME FOR NAGARE BECAUSE I WAS WEARING HIS YUKATA.
SHLUK
BLUBLUP
SO THAT'S HOW YOU GOT SOAKED.

SHE WAS SO STRONG. YOU'D NEVER HAVE KNOWN SHE WAS A WOMAN.
Darn! I dropped my glasses.
I USED MY SHADE MAGIC AND MANAGED TO ESCAPE.

Lately a lot of people have been asking me where they should send their letters. So here you go.

Attn:
Yoko Matsushita
Hana to Yume
Editorial Department
2-2-2 Awajicho,
Kanda, Chiyoda-ku
Tokyo, Japan

Please send them there. As long as we're on the subject, I'd like to talk a little about the letters you send me. I get a lot of letters saying, "Please draw me a picture of this," or "Send me your autograph." Please don't ask me for drawings. I just don't have the time. It's hard enough for me to finish my manga. I can't sign autographs either. Some people write, "I've got to have your autograph"—they're always the ones who don't include a stamp or an envelope for me (laugh). And of course people who say, "You have to write me back"—they don't include envelopes either (laugh). If you're going to demand a response, then it's just good manners to include a self-addressed stamped envelope. I try to respond to people who include a stamp, but sometimes I'm just too busy. Please be aware of that. That's all for now.

ARE YOU SURE IT WAS A REAL GHOST?
I THINK I CAN TELL THE DIFFERENCE BETWEEN A HUMAN BEING AND A GHOST, THANK YOU VERY MUCH.
I'm not without some spirit power.

AND SHE WAS A LOCATION-BOUND GHOST!!
Just like that old scary TV show "The Unknown World."
Wow!
SUPER-SERIOUS

Wasn't he scared witless just a second ago?

STILL ...
THERE IS ONE THING I HAVEN'T FIGURED OUT.
WHAT THE GHOST SAID...

THE WAY SHE WAS TALKING ...
IT WAS ALMOST LIKE...

...A WIFE TALKING TO HER HUS-BAND.
I WOVE THAT YUKATA ...

BE CAREFUL YOU DON'T CATCH A COLD.
SOUNDS LIKE THIS JOB IS GOING TO TAKE A WHILE.
We've got a long way to go.
ALL RIGHT.

WATARI...
YEAH?

I'VE A FAVOR TO ASK YOU.

Ministry of Hades, Area Five: The Judgment Bureau
WORK WORK
HOW'S IT GOING AT YOUR END, ANI?
I GUESS THIS ABOUT WRAPS IT UP.
Sigh...
WE'RE ALREADY SO BUSY, AND TATSUMI ASKED US TO DO THESE IMPOSSIBLE TASKS.
HOW TRUE.
WHAT DID TATSUMI ASK YOU TO DO?
DOOM

HEY
Te--
TERAZUMA?!
What are you doing here?
WHAT ARE YOU SO SHAKEN UP ABOUT?
A month overdue →
THE VULUNA PICTURE BOOK
THANK...
...YOU.
...
HERE'S THE BOOK I BORROWED.
What the heck were you doing with that, Hajime?
I'm glad you returned it, but next time come when the library is actually open!!
There's no smoking in here!!
Now, now.
HEY! WHAT'S THIS?
IT'S ALL DATA ON THE IMAGINARY WORLD.
IS THAT WHAT TATSUMI ASKED YOU FOR?
YES.
(MESSY)

A WHILE BACK, A SHIISAA FELL THROUGH A WORMHOLE INTO OKINAWA, RIGHT?
YOU KNOW ABOUT THE GHOSE AT THE INN?
YEAH.
THE THING THAT CHIDSURU TOOK IN AND IS RAISING.
That thing.
FWUMP
Smoking is prohibited here, Hajime.
LATELY, THE IMAGINARY WORLD HAS BEEN VERY UNSTABLE AND WORM-HOLES KEEP APPEARING.
TATSUMI ASKED US TO GATHER INFORMATION IN CASE IT HAPPENS AGAIN.
HMM...
HE'S A SMART GUY.

STILL, I DON'T THINK WE HAVE TO WORRY ABOUT SHIKI FALLING THROUGH EVERY WORM-HOLE THAT OPENS UP.
THIS IS JUST A PRECAU-TION.
HEY, GUSHO-SHIN!
I'M THIRSTY.
MAKE ME SOME COFFEE.
A cup of joe.
I just got done working out.
Lifting weights
WHAM
GRRRR
THEN WHY DON'T YOU DRINK SOME WATER AND GO TO BED, FOOL?!!
WHUMP
GEEZ!!! ALL THAT JERK EVER DOES IS PESTER ME!!!
huff huff
IT IS RATHER LATE.
LET'S CALL IT A NIGHT.

BEEP
AN E-MAIL.

Ah!
TH-THAT ADDRESS!
IT'S TATSUMI !!

Uh-oh.
I HAVE A BAD FEELING ABOUT THIS.
I'll deal with it tomorrow.
BUT IT LOOKS URGENT.

WIP
LET'S SEE...

WHUP

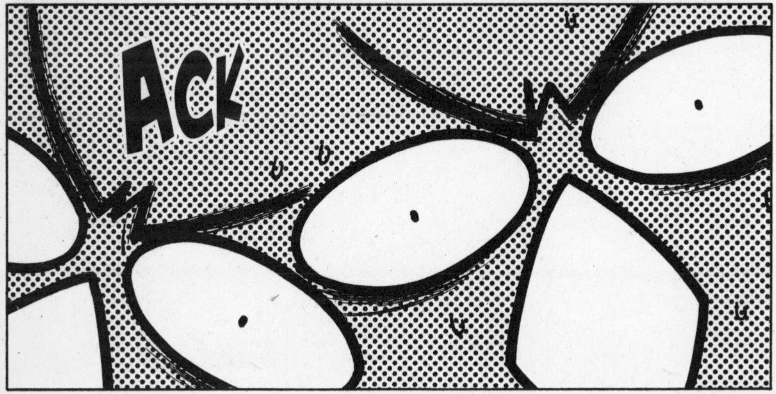
ACK

件名 大至急
削除
ファイル
すぐに送信
スケジュールしない
署名を使用
追加
削除
種類
差出人
アドレス
koganemusi

JUDGMENT BUREAU LIBRARIANS

URGENT: PLEASE SEND DATA REGARDING THE SUBJECTS BELOW.

※TIMES AND PLACES THAT WORMHOLES HAVE APPEARED IN THE IMAGINARY WORLD.

※THE RESULTS OF ALL INVESTIGATIONS REGARDING WORMHOLES.

WHAT THE...

SOAKING

plip plip

OH MY...

WHAT'S GOING ON?

OINK

IT WOULD BE RUDE OF ME TO RETURN THIS WHILE IT'S STILL WET.
HMM... HMM... HMM...
And it is Nagare's yukata.
BUT WE DON'T HAVE THE FUNDS TO BUY HIM A NEW ONE.
HMM...
What a fancy yukata. How decadent. That's exactly why I can't stand these famous old families.
...
MAYBE I COULD JUST NOT MENTION IT.
HEH HEH HEH
TWINKLE
EVIL
FLASH!
?!!
So bright!
LIGHT?

KLAK
KLAK
...
KLAK
WHAT ARE YOU DOING, MIYA?
DOOM
!!!

OH...
SORRY, DID I STARTLE YOU?
OH, TATSUMI.
A LITTLE BIT.

SO YOU'RE BACK.
FWUP

ORGANIZING THE STORAGE AREA AT THIS TIME OF NIGHT?
YES.
I'M GOING TO AIR IT OUT TOMORROW, SO I'M STRAIGHTENING UP.
KLAK KLAK

IT'S SO MEAN!
THE OTHERS MADE ME DO THIS ALL BY MYSELF!!
It's my punishment for winning the lottery.
Ha ha...
CAN I GIVE YOU A HAND?
WHAT?!
REALLY?

THANK YOU!
THIS PLACE IS SO FAR FROM THE MAIN HOUSE AND IT'S SO DARK. IT'S SCARY TO BE HERE ALL ALONE!
OF COURSE.
I OWE YOU ONE, MIYA.
SMILE
BESIDES...
...
WHO KNOWS WHAT I'LL DISCOVER?
What's with that background?

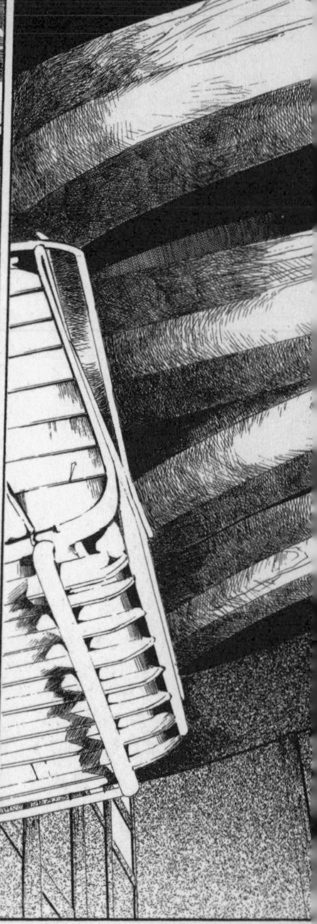

?

黒崎

WHAT'S THIS?
THE KURO-SAKI FAMILY TREE.
SO THAT'S WHERE IT WAS.

黒崎
THE KUROSAKI FAMILY TREE...

MAY I HAVE A LOOK?
I DON'T THINK ANYONE WOULD MIND.
IF IT WERE IMPORTANT, IT WOULD BE IN THE MASTER'S ROOM.

CWUP
HMM...
ALL THE NAMES ARE JUST ONE CHARACTER.
I wonder if that was a rule.
THEY FOLLOW REN'S NAMING CONVENTION.
雫 (SHIZUKU)
南 (MINAMI)
(KAI)
第十六代当主
流 (NAGARE)
(MASTER OF 16TH GENERATION)
厳 (GEN)
密 (HISOKA)
HMM...
It's so dark.
It's hard to read.
VEEN
WHAT?!
A WOMAN WAS THE MASTER OF THIS GENERATION.
THAT'S UNUSUAL IN SAMURAI FAMILIES.
第五代当主
紫 (MURASAKI)
(MASTER OF 5TH GENERATION)
葵 (AOI)
WHAT? THAT CAN'T BE!

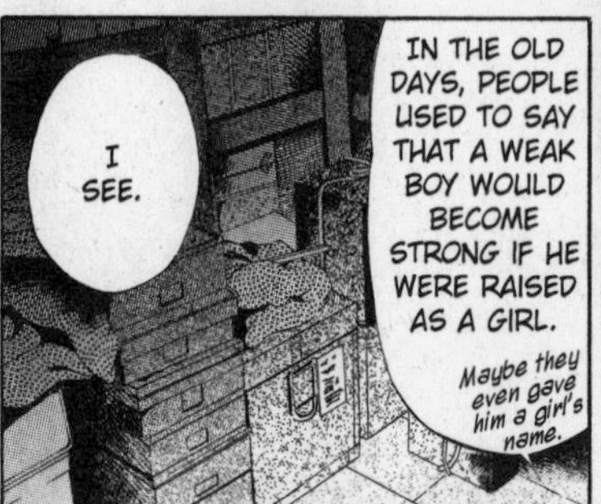

Well, it is an old family.

?!
THERE'S SOMETHING...
...STRANGE...
月
(TSUKI)
蛍
雫
(SHIZUKU)
南
第十四代当主
(MASTER OF 14TH GENERATION)
...
...ABOUT THIS FAMILY TREE.
流
第十六代当
(MASTER OF 16TH GENERATION)
BUT WHAT IS IT?
?!
KOFF KOFF KOFF

KOFF KOFF
KOFF
UNGH!
Haa...
GASP!
GASP...
SPLAT
AH...
UNH...
HEH HEH HEH...
KOFF
POOR NAGARE.
UNH ...
THOOM
UNH ...
...BECAUSE OF THE SINS OF YOUR ANCESTOR, YOUR BODY IS MINE...IF NOT YOUR SOUL.
AGH ...
SH-SHUT UP, YOU MONSTER!
MY DARLING, MY WRETCHED LITTLE PLAYTHING ...

SHUP SHUP
HEH HEH HEH... THAT'S QUITE A FORKED TONGUE YOU'VE GOT, NAGARE.
BUT YOUR FATHER AND YOUR GRANDFATHER... AND EVERYONE WHO SHARES THAT BASTARD'S BLOOD...
SWISH
SHUP
...MUST GROVEL BEFORE ME!!!
SHLUK
GLUP
UH... AH... AAH...
AHH... ISN'T THIS DELIGHT-FUL? I CAN HARDLY STAND IT!
S-Stop it!
AH...THE JOY OF SOILING SUCH A NOBLE SOUL.
Huff Huff
IT'S AS DELIGHT-FUL AS DEFILING A SAINT.
AAH!!
YES, GROVEL! GROVEL!! IF YOU RESIST, YOU'LL ONLY SUFFER MORE!
Huff
UNH ...
SHLUK

IF YOU'LL JUST RELAX AND GIVE YOUR BODY OVER TO ME, THE PAIN WILL GO AWAY.
DON'T YOU WANT TO BE FREE?
GLUP
DON'T YOU JUST WANT TO ATTACH YOURSELF TO MY BODY SO BADLY YOU CAN HARDLY HELP YOURSELF?
Huff
YOU PIECE OF FILTH!!!
N...
NO!
Huff
Huff
AAH ...
YOU'RE AN OBSCENITY...
Huff
Huff
SHLUK
GRAH
HOW DARE YOU DEFAME MY ANCESTORS!
LOOK AT YOU. YOU'RE AS CLUMSY AND PATHETIC AS HE WAS.
SHUT UP!!!

YOUR ANCESTOR ...THAT MAN... KILLED ME WHILE IN HUMAN FORM!!
Unh...
Ung...
Unh...
SHAKE
SHAKE
UNH ...
SHAKE
SHAKE
Sh...
SHUT UP! WE KILLED YOU FOR THE SAKE OF THIS VILLAGE!
Gasp...
UNH ...
AAAH! AAAH!!
WHAT A DESPICABLE, WICKED LINEAGE!!!
HA HA HA HA... AND WHAT DID YOUR DEAR VILLAGERS DO IN RETURN?
huff
huff
huff
AAH
SWUP
AAAAH!!

FWUP
THE ONLY REASON THEY STILL HOLD THE FESTIVAL IN HONOR OF THE "HEROIC GOD-KILLER" IS TO SEAL MY CURSE INTO THE KUROSAKI BLOODLINE.

"IT WAS ONLY ONE FAMILY THAT KILLED YOU."

...

"IF YOU MUST CURSE SOMEONE, PLEASE CURSE ONLY THEM."

"WE BEG YOU, YATONO-KAMI!"
SHUT UP!
HEH HEH HEH... HA HA HA... ISN'T THAT AMUSING?
SHUT UP!
SHUT UP!
IF A REAL HERO WERE TO HEAR YOU NOW, HE'D BE DISGUSTED.
YOUR FAMILY WAS OFFERED AS A SACRIFICE BY THIS VILLAGE.
Heh heh...
DLIP DLIP
UNH... UNNNH...
HA HA HA HA HA HA!!

SHLIP
I WILL NEVER BE DESTROYED !!!
AHH
UGH
I WILL ALWAYS BE LURKING IN YOUR BLOOD UNTIL THE TIME WHEN YOUR FAMILY FINALLY DIES OUT...
AAAAH!!!
SHLUK
AND ON THAT DAY...
UNH
...I WILL RISE AGAIN.
BLUP BLUP
GACK
BA-BUMP BA-BUMP
UNH...
AH...

End of Descendants of Darkness Book 11

Life As An Angel Can Be Hell

With a bad temper, a broken home, and an un-holy attraction to his sister, Setsuna is no angel. But he used to be – literally. Reincarnated as a teenage boy, creatures from heaven and hell soon come to him, each with their own agendas. Whose side will Setsuna choose?

The inspiration for the OAV, now available for the first time in English. Start your graphic novel collection today!

Only $9.95!

Angel Sanctuary™

Tenshi Kinryou Ku © Kaori Yuki 1994/HAKUSENSHA, Inc.

www.viz.com
store.viz.com

VIZ MEDIA